ACCOUNTING RAPID KICK-START FOR BEGINNERS

A Comprehensive Guide to Simplified Financial & Managerial Accounting for Students, Business Owners, and Finance Professionals

JOEY HANA

Copyright © 2024 by Joey Hana

All rights reserved.

No part of this work may be reproduced, distributed, or transmitted in any form or by any means, including photocopying, recording, or other electronic or mechanical methods, without the prior written permission of the author, except in the case of brief quotations embodied in critical reviews and certain other noncommercial uses permitted by copyright law.

Table of Contents

INTRODUCTION TO ACCOUNTING

CHAPTER ONE: THE BASICS: UNDERSTANDING FINANCIAL STATEMENTS

CHAPTER TWO: MASTERING THE BALANCE SHEET

CHAPTER THREE: DECODING THE INCOME STATEMENT

CHAPTER FOUR: BUDGETING ESSENTIALS

CHAPTER FIVE: PERFORMANCE MEASUREMENT AND EVALUATION

CHAPTER SIX: CASE STUDIES AND PRACTICAL APPLICATIONS

CONCLUSION: YOUR ACCOUNTING JOURNEY AHEAD

INTRODUCTION TO ACCOUNTING

This book is a comprehensive guide designed to simplify financial and managerial accounting for various audiences, including students, business owners, and finance professionals. It covers the fundamental principles and practices of accounting, providing a quick and accessible introduction to key concepts such as financial statements, budgeting, cost analysis, and more. Whether you're just starting or looking to refresh your knowledge, this book offers a streamlined approach to understanding accounting essentials.

Accounting is the language of business. It is a systematic process of recording, summarizing, analyzing, and interpreting financial information. Whether you are a student, a business owner, or a finance professional, understanding accounting is essential for making informed financial decisions.

Financial Accounting focuses on the preparation and presentation of financial statements that are used by external stakeholders, such as investors, creditors, and government agencies, to assess the financial health of an organization. These financial statements include the income statement, balance sheet, statement of cash flows, and statement of changes in equity.

The income statement provides a summary of revenues, expenses, gains, and losses over a specific period, typically a month, quarter, or year. It shows the profitability of a business by calculating the net income or net loss.

The balance sheet presents the financial position of a company at a specific point in time. It consists of three main components: assets, liabilities, and equity. Assets are the resources owned by a company, while liabilities represent its obligations. Equity represents the residual interest in the assets after deducting liabilities.

The statement of cash flows tracks the cash inflows and outflows during a given period. It categorizes cash flows into operating, investing, and financing activities, providing insights into how cash is generated and used within the organization.

The statement of changes in equity shows the changes in equity accounts over a particular timeframe. It reflects the contributions from shareholders, distributions to shareholders, and other factors affecting equity.

Managerial Accounting, on the other hand, focuses on providing internal users, such as managers and employees, with relevant financial information to support decision-making, planning, and control within an organization. Managerial accounting reports may include budgets, cost analysis, performance reports, and variance analysis.

By the end of this comprehensive guide, you will have a solid understanding of both financial and managerial accounting concepts. You will be able to interpret financial statements, make informed financial decisions, and effectively communicate financial information.

Remember, accounting is a practical skill that requires practice and application. Embrace the learning process, and don't hesitate to seek clarification or additional resources when needed. Let's embark on this accounting journey together, and I'm confident that you will gain the knowledge and skills necessary to excel in the world of finance.

CHAPTER ONE: THE BASICS: UNDERSTANDING FINANCIAL STATEMENTS

In this chapter, we will explore the fascinating world of accounting and help you build a solid foundation in financial and managerial accounting.

Accounting is like the language of business. It helps us understand how well a company is doing financially. Whether you're a student, business owner, or finance expert, knowing about accounting is super important for making smart decisions.

Understanding financial statements is like deciphering the heartbeat of a business. It's about unveiling the story behind the numbers, from the balance sheet revealing assets and liabilities to the income statement painting a picture of profitability. Dive into the world of finance, where numbers speak volumes, and learn to decode the language of financial statements to make informed decisions and drive success.

Let's start by understanding the basics of financial statements.

Financial statements are like reports that tell us about a company's money situation. They show us things like how much money they're making, what they own, what they owe, and where their money is going.

The first financial statement we'll explore is the income statement. Think of this as a report card for a company's money-making. It shows how much money they brought in, how much they spent, and if they made a profit or loss.

Next, we have the balance sheet. This one gives us a snapshot of what a company owns and owes at a specific time. It's like looking at their belongings (assets), debts (liabilities), and what's left over (equity). It helps us see how stable the company is financially.

Moving on, we have the statement of cash flows. This statement tells us where a company's money is coming from and where it's going. It breaks down cash activities into three main parts: operating, investing, and financing. Operating activities include cash generated from day-to-day operations, such as sales revenue and payments to suppliers. Investing activities involve cash flows related to investments in assets or the sale of assets. Financing activities include cash flows from borrowing or repaying loans, issuing or buying back shares, and paying dividends. The statement of cash flows provides insights into how a company manages its cash and where it's coming from or going.

Lastly, we have the statement of changes in equity. This statement shows how a company's equity changes over a specific period. It reflects the contributions from shareholders, distributions to shareholders, and other factors affecting equity. By analyzing this statement, we can understand the changes in the ownership interests of the company.

Understanding these financial statements is vital because they allow us to assess a company's financial health, performance, and cash flow. They provide us with valuable information to make informed decisions about investing, lending, or doing business with a company.

Remember, accounting is a skill that requires practice and application. It gets easier with time and effort. Embrace the learning process, ask questions, and seek additional resources when needed.

CHAPTER TWO: MASTERING THE BALANCE SHEET

Now, let's delve into one of the essential financial statements: the balance sheet. The balance sheet provides a snapshot of a company's financial position at a specific moment in time. It's like taking a picture of the company's financial health.

Imagine you're examining a balance sheet as if you were peering through a window into the company's financial world. The balance sheet has three main components: assets, liabilities, and equity.

Assets represent what the company owns. These can include cash, inventory, buildings, equipment, and investments. Assets are the resources that help the company generate revenue and operate its business.

Liabilities, on the other hand, are the company's obligations or debts. They can include loans, accounts payable (money owed to suppliers), and other liabilities. Liabilities reflect the claims that others have on the company's assets.

Equity represents the residual interest in the company's assets after deducting liabilities. It represents the owners' stake in the business. Equity can come from various sources, such as initial investments by the owners and retained earnings (profits reinvested in the company).

To understand the balance sheet better, let's use an analogy. Imagine you have a jar. The jar represents the company, and the contents represent its assets. Now, fill the jar with different items, representing cash, inventory, equipment, and other assets. These items reflect what the company owns.

Now, let's move to the lid of the jar. It has two sections: one for liabilities and one for equity. Imagine pouring different colored marbles into the sections. The marbles in the liability section represent the company's debts and obligations, while the marbles in the equity section represent the owners' investments and retained earnings.

Here's the fascinating part: the balance sheet always balances. Just like the name suggests, the total value of assets should equal the total of liabilities and equity. If you take out one marble from the liability section, you need to take out a marble from the equity section to keep the balance.

Analyzing the balance sheet can provide valuable insights into a company's financial strength and stability. For example, a company with a large amount of cash and valuable assets may be in a strong position to meet its obligations. On the other hand, a company with significant liabilities compared to its assets might be facing financial challenges.

By understanding the balance sheet, you can assess a company's financial health, evaluate its ability to repay debts, and even compare it to other companies in the same industry.

But the balance sheet is more than just a static report – it's a dynamic tool that evolves with every transaction your business makes. Understanding how these transactions impact the balance sheet is crucial for effective financial management. For example, when you purchase new equipment using a loan, your assets increase, but so do your liabilities. Conversely, when you generate revenue and retain profits, your equity grows, strengthening your financial position.

Mastering the balance sheet empowers you to make informed decisions about resource allocation, debt management, and investment strategies. It enables you to identify areas of strength and weakness, allowing you to capitalize on opportunities and mitigate risks. Whether you're a student seeking a solid foundation in accounting or a business owner navigating the complexities of financial management, grasping the balance sheet is a vital step toward achieving your goals.

So, embrace the challenge of mastering the balance sheet, and unlock a world of financial knowledge that will serve you well throughout your personal and professional endeavors. With a deep understanding of this powerful tool, you'll be equipped to steer your financial ship toward prosperous waters.

Remember, mastering the balance sheet takes practice and familiarity with different types of assets, liabilities, and equity. As you progress through this guide, we will provide you with practical examples and real-world scenarios to enhance your understanding.

So, let's continue our journey of mastering accounting by exploring the balance sheet further. Get ready to unlock valuable insights into a company's financial position and gain the confidence to make informed decisions in the world of finance.

CHAPTER THREE: DECODING THE INCOME STATEMENT

Let's dive into another important financial statement: the income statement. It gives us a snapshot of a company's financial performance over a set period, whether it's a month, quarter, or year. Think of it like peeking through a window to see how the company's doing financially.

The income statement is like a story that shows whether the company is making money or facing challenges. It has three main parts: revenues, expenses, and the resulting profit or loss.

Revenues, also called sales, show how much money the company makes from selling its stuff or services. They're crucial for keeping the business going and can come from different sources like selling goods or services.

Expenses represent the costs of running the business and making revenue. These can include things like buying materials, paying employees, rent, and marketing. Expenses are like the necessary ingredient you need to make your business work.

Now, let's add up the revenues and subtract the expenses. The result is the company's net income, or profit. If revenues are more than expenses, the company's making a profit, which means it's doing well financially. But if expenses are more than revenues, the company faces a loss, indicating some financial trouble.

Looking at the income statement helps us understand how well a company's doing financially, whether it's making money, and if it's a good investment.

Let's simplify it even more with an analogy. Imagine you're baking a cake. The stuff you buy, like flour and eggs, are expenses. They're what you need to make the final product—the cake you sell, which is the revenue.

The income statement helps you see if your cake business is profitable. If the money from selling cakes is more than what you spent on ingredients and other stuff, you're making a profit. But if your costs are more than what you earn, you're facing a loss, and you might need to adjust your business plan.

As you dig into the income statement, you'll see lots of expenses—the investments you make to keep your business running. From the cost of goods to operational expenses, each one is carefully recorded, showing you where your money's going.

But the real magic happens when you start to analyze how these expenses and revenues relate. With each dollar earned and spent, you learn more about your business's profitability and efficiency. By understanding these relationships, you can find areas to improve and make smarter decisions to grow your business.

So, embrace the challenge of understanding the income statement, and use its insights to take your business to new heights. With this knowledge, you'll be ready to make informed decisions and leave an indelible mark on the world of commerce.

CHAPTER FOUR: BUDGETING ESSENTIALS

Budgeting is like plotting a course for your finances—it's your roadmap to financial success. It's not just about jotting down what you spend; it's about planning your financial journey. Here's how to make budgeting both practical and enjoyable:

1. Know Your Goals: First things first, figure out what you want to achieve with your money. Whether it's saving up for a vacation, buying a house, or paying off

debt, having clear goals gives you direction.

2. Track Your Money: Keep an eye on what's coming in and what's going out. This helps you understand your spending habits and find areas where you can save.

3. Create Categories: Sort your expenses into categories like rent, food, bills, transport, fun stuff, and savings. This makes it easier to see where your money is being allocated.

4. Set Limits: Once you know where your money's going, set boundaries for each

category. Be realistic, but also challenge yourself to cut back where you can.

5. Emergency Fund: Always keep some money aside for emergencies. Life is full of surprises and having a safety net can ease your mind when unexpected expenses pop up.

6. Check In Regularly: Budgeting's not a one-time deal—it's an ongoing process. Take some time every month to review your budget and make adjustments as needed.

7. Use Technology: Use apps and online tools to make budgeting easier. Many

apps automatically sort your spending and give you insights into your habits.

8. Stay Motivated: Celebrate your success, big or small. Whether it's sticking to your budget for a month or hitting a savings goal, keeping your eyes on the prize can keep you motivated, even when budgeting gets tough.

By following these simple steps, you can take control of your finances and work towards a brighter financial future.

CHAPTER FIVE: PERFORMANCE MEASUREMENT AND EVALUATION

Performance measurement and evaluation act like your compass and map on your journey to success. They're there to keep you on course, help you tweak your plans, and ultimately reach your goals. Let's break it down with a simple story:

Imagine you're a chef getting ready for a big cooking contest. You've spent weeks getting your recipes just right, but how do you know if you're ready to win? Well, that's where performance measurement and evaluation step in.

As you cook, you taste each dish, checking the flavors, textures, and how it looks on the plate. You also keep an eye on the clock, making sure you're keeping up with the competition's schedule. With each taste and glance at the clock, you figure out what you can do better and adjust as needed.

But it's not just about your own opinion. You also listen to what the judges and other chefs have to say. Their feedback helps you understand how your dishes are being received and where you can shine even more.

In the end, it's not just about winning the contest; it's about getting better at what you do. Performance measurement and evaluation show you the way to keep improving, guiding you toward becoming an even greater chef.

Just like in the kitchen, in anything you do, keeping track of how you're doing and evaluating the results is key to success. They give you the knowledge you need to make smart choices, refine your plans, and, ultimately, reach your dreams.

CHAPTER SIX: CASE STUDIES AND PRACTICAL APPLICATIONS

Case studies and practical examples are like real-life stories that make concepts come alive and show how they're useful in the real world. Let me give you an example:

Imagine you're a marketing manager getting ready to launch a new product in a competitive market. You've studied textbooks and been to seminars, but now it's time to put what you've learned into action.

You look at a case study of a similar product launch from a few years back. By looking at what worked and what didn't, you get useful insights into the challenges you might face and the strategies that could help you succeed.

With this knowledge, you create a detailed marketing plan. You include things like targeted advertising, teaming up with influencers, and using social media. But you don't just stop there; you keep an eye on how things are going, making changes based on what you see and hear.

As the launch gets closer, you're excited and nervous. But because you learned from the case study and were proactive about putting it into action, the launch goes amazingly well. Sales go up, and soon everyone knows about your product.

This story shows how looking at real-world examples and using what you learn can help you make smart choices and get real results in any field or industry.

CONCLUSION: YOUR ACCOUNTING JOURNEY AHEAD

Congratulations on starting your accounting journey! This guide has all you need to begin understanding financial and managerial accounting, whether you're a student, business owner, or finance professional.

We've made complex accounting concepts easy to understand, so even beginners can get it. From learning the basics of financial statements to mastering cost analysis and budgeting, you now have a solid foundation to build upon.

Just remember, the key to mastering accounting is to keep learning and practicing. As you go along, don't be afraid to dig into more resources like textbooks, online classes, or getting advice from professional mentors.

Whether you're pursuing a career in finance, managing your own business, or simply striving for financial literacy, accounting is a valuable skill that will serve you well. Embrace the challenges, celebrate your victories, and keep exploring the world of accounting—it's fascinating!

Your path might have lots of numbers and spreadsheets, but with focus and dedication, you'll unlock the power of accounting to make smart financial choices and find success. Here's to your journey ahead—may it be full of growth and triumph!

www.ingramcontent.com/pod-product-compliance
Lightning Source LLC
Chambersburg PA
CBHW070950220526
45471CB00007B/2975